Alexander Johnston

Representative American Orations to Illustrate American Political History

Vol. 3

Alexander Johnston

Representative American Orations to Illustrate American Political History
Vol. 3

ISBN/EAN: 9783337068721

Printed in Europe, USA, Canada, Australia, Japan

Cover: Foto ©Suzi / pixelio.de

More available books at **www.hansebooks.com**

REPRESENTATIVE
AMERICAN ORATIONS

TO ILLUSTRATE

AMERICAN POLITICAL HISTORY

EDITED, WITH INTRODUCTIONS

BY

ALEXANDER JOHNSTON

PROFESSOR OF JURISPRUDENCE AND POLITICAL ECONOMY IN THE
COLLEGE OF NEW JERSEY

NEW YORK & LONDON

G. P. PUTNAM'S SONS

The Knickerbocker Press

1884

CONTENTS.

CONTENTS. v

V.

THE ANTI-SLAVERY STRUGGLE.

(CONTINUED FROM VOLUME II.)

ABRAHAM LINCOLN,

OF ILLINOIS.

(BORN 1809, DIED 1865.)

ON HIS NOMINATION TO THE UNITED STATES SEN-
ATE, AT THE REPUBLICAN STATE CONVENTION,
SPRINGFIELD, ILLS., JUNE 17, 1858.

MR. PRESIDENT AND GENTLEMEN OF THE
CONVENTION:

If we could first know where we are, and
whither we are tending, we could better judge
what to do, and how to do it. We are now
far into the fifth year since a policy was initiated
with the avowed object, and confident promise,
of putting an end to slavery agitation. Under
the operation of that policy, that agitation not
only has not ceased, but has constantly aug-
mented. In my opinion, it will not cease until
a crisis shall have been reached and passed. "A
house divided against itself cannot stand." I
believe this Government cannot endure permanently half slave and half free. I do not ex-

pect the Union to be dissolved ; I do not expect the house to fall; but I do expect that it will cease to be divided. It will become all one thing, or all the other. Either the opponents of slavery will arrest the further spread of it, and place it where the public mind shall rest in the belief that it is in the course of ultimate extinction; or its advocates will push it forward till it shall become alike lawful in all the States, old and new, North as well as South. Have we no tendency to the latter condition? Let any one who doubts carefully contemplate that now almost complete legal combination-piece of machinery, so to speak—compounded of the Nebraska doctrine and the Dred Scott decision. Let him consider not only what work the machinery is adapted to do, and how well adapted, but also let him study the history of its construction, and trace, if he can, or rather fail, if he can, to trace the evidences of design and concert of action among its chief architects from the beginning.

The new year of 1854 found slavery excluded from more than half the States by State constitutions, and from most of the national territory by Congressional prohibition. Four days later commenced the struggle which ended in repealing that Congressional prohibition. This opened all the national territory to slavery, and was the first point gained. But, so far, Congress only had acted, and an indorsement, by the people, real or apparent, was indispensable, to save the point already gained and give chance for more. This necessity had not been overlooked, but had been provided for, as well as might be, in the notable argument of "squatter sovereignty," otherwise called "sacred right of self-government";—which latter phrase though expressive of the only rightful basis of any government, was so perverted in this attempted use of it as to amount to just this: That, if any *one* man choose to enslave *another*, no *third* man shall be allowed to object. That argument was incorporated with the Nebraska bill itself, in the language which follows: "It being the true intent and meaning of this act, not to legislate slavery into any Territory or State, nor to exclude it therefrom ; but to leave the people thereof perfectly free to form and regulate their domestic institutions in their own way, subject only to the Constitution of the United States." Then opened the roar of loose declamation in favor of "squatter sovereignty," and "sacred right of self-government." "But," said opposition members, "let us amend the bill so as to expressly declare that the people of the Territory *may* exclude slavery." "Not we," said the friends of the measure; and down they voted the amendment.

While the Nebraska bill was passing through Congress, a *law-case*, involving the question of a negro's freedom, by reason of his owner having voluntarily taken him first into a free State, and then into a Territory covered by the Congressional prohibition, and held him as a slave for a long time in each, was passing through the United States Circuit Court for the District of Missouri; and both Nebraska bill and lawsuit were brought to a decision in the same month of May, 1854. The negro's name was Dred Scott, which name now designates the decision finally made in the case. Before the then next Presidential election, the law-case came to, and was argued in, the Supreme Court of the United States; but the decision of it was deferred until after the election. Still, before the election, Senator Trumbull, on the floor of the Senate, requested the leading advocate of the Nebraska bill to state his *opinion* whether the people of a Territory can constitutionally exclude slavery from their limits; and the latter answers: "That is a question for the Supreme Court."

The election came, Mr. Buchanan was elected, and the indorsement, such as it was, secured. That was the second point gained. * * * The Supreme Court met again, did not announce their decision, but ordered a re-argument. The Presidential inauguration came, and still no decision of the court; but the incoming President, in his inaugural address, fervently exhorted the people to abide by the forthcoming decision, whatever it might be. Then, in a few days, came the decision. The reputed author of the Nebraska bill finds an early occasion to make a speech at this capital, indorsing the Dred Scott decision, and vehemently denouncing all opposition to it. The new President, too, seizes the early occasion of the Silliman letter to indorse and strongly construe that decision, and to express his astonishment that any different view had ever been entertained.

At length a squabble springs up between the President and the author of the Nebraska bill, on the mere question of fact, whether the Lecompton constitution was, or was not, in any just sense, made by the people of Kansas; and in that quarrel the latter declares that all he

wants is a fair vote for the people, and that he
cares not whether slavery be voted *down* or
voted *up*. I do not understand his declaration,
that he cares not whether slavery be voted
down or voted up, to be intended by him other
than as an apt definition of the policy he would
impress upon the public mind—the principle
for which he declares he has suffered so much,
and is ready to suffer to the end. And well
may he cling to that principle. If he has any
parental feeling, well may he cling to it. That
principle is the only shred left of his original
Nebraska doctrine. Under the Dred Scott decision, squatter sovereignty squatted out of
existence—tumbled down like temporary scaffolding—like the mould at the foundry, served
through one blast, and fell back into loose
sand,—helped to carry an election, and then
was kicked to the winds.   *   *   *

The several points of the Dred Scot decision,
in connection with Senator Douglas' " care-
not " policy, constitute the piece of machinery
in its present state of advancement. This was
the third point gained. The working points of
that machinery are: (1) That no negro slave,
imported as such from Africa, and no descend-
ant of such slave, can ever be a citizen of any

State, in the sense of that term as used in the Constitution of the United States. This point is made in order to deprive the negro, in every possible event, of the benefit of that provision of the United States Constitution, which declares that "the citizens of each State shall be entitled to all privileges and immunities of citizens in the several States." (2) That, "subject to the Constitution of the United States," neither Congress nor a Territorial Legislature can exclude slavery from any United States Territory. This point is made in order that individual men may fill up the Territories with slaves, without danger of losing them as property, and thus to enhance the chances of permanency to the institution through all the future. (3) That whether the holding a negro in actual slavery in a free State makes him free, as against the holder, the United States courts will not decide, but will leave to be decided by the courts of any slave State the negro may be forced into by the master. This point is made, not to be pressed immediately; but, if acquiesced in for a while, and apparently indorsed by the people at an election, then to sustain the logical conclusion that what Dred Scott's master might lawfully do with Dred Scott, in the

State of Illinois, every other master may lawfully do with any other one or one thousand slaves, in Illinois, or in any other free State.

Auxiliary to all this, and working hand in hand with it, the Nebraska doctrine, or what is left of it, is to educate and mould public opinion, at least Northern public opinion, not to care whether slavery is voted down or voted up. This shows exactly where we now are, and partially, also, whither we are tending.

It will throw additional light on the latter to go back, and run the mind over the string of historical facts already stated. Several things will now appear less dark and mysterious than they did when they were transpiring. The people were to be left "perfectly free." "subject only to the Constitution." What the Constitution had to do with it, outsiders could not then see. Plainly enough now, it was an exactly fitted niche for the Dred Scott decision to come in afterward, and declare the perfect freedom of the people to be just no freedom at all. * * * Why was the court decision held up? Why even a Senator's individual opinion withheld till after the Presidential election? Plainly enough now: the speaking out then would have damaged the perfectly free argument upon which the election was to be carried. Why the outgoing President's felicitation on the indorsement? Why the delay of a re-argument? Why the incoming President's advance exhortation in favor of the decision? These things look like the cautious patting and petting of a spirited horse preparatory to mounting him, when it is dreaded that he may give the rider a fall. * * *

We cannot absolutely know that all these exact adaptations are the result of preconcert. But when we see a lot of framed timbers, different portions of which we know have been gotten out at different times and places, and by different workmen—Stephen, Franklin, Roger, and James, for instance,—and when we see these timbers joined together, and see that they exactly make the frame of a house or a mill, all the tenons and mortices exactly fitting, and all the lengths and proportions of the different pieces exactly adapted to their respective places, and not a piece too many or too few—not omitting even scaffolding,—or, if a single piece be lacking, we see the place in the frame exactly fitted and prepared yet to bring such piece in, —in such a case, we find it impossible not to believe that Stephen and Franklin and Roger and James all understood one another from the beginning, and all worked upon a common plan or draft drawn up before the first blow was struck.

It should not be overlooked that, by the Nebraska bill, the people of a *State*, as well as Territory, were to be left "perfectly free," "subject only to the Constitution." Why mention a State? They were legislating for Territories, and not for or about States. Certainly, the people of a State are and ought to be subject to the Constitution of the United States; but why is mention of this lugged into this merely Territorial law? Why are the people of a Territory and the people of a State therein lumped together, and their relation to the Constitution therein treated as being precisely the same? While the opinion of the court, by Chief-Justice Taney, in the Dred Scott case, and the separate opinions of all the concurring judges, expressly declare that the Constitution of the United States permits neither Congress nor a Territorial Legislature to exclude slavery from any United States Territory, they all omit to declare whether or not the same Constitution permits a State, or the people of a State, to exclude it. *Possibly*, this is a mere omission. * * * The nearest approach to the point of declaring the power of a State over slavery is made by Judge Nelson. He approaches it more than once, using the precise idea, and almost the language, too, of the Nebraska act. On one occasion, his exact language is : " Except in cases when the power is restrained by the Constitution of the United States, the law of the State is supreme over the subjects of slavery within its jurisdiction." In what cases the power of the States is so restrained by the United States Constitution is left an open question, precisely as the same question, as to the restraint on the power of the Territories, was left open in the Nebraska act. Put this and that together, and we have another nice little niche, which we may, erelong, see filled with another Supreme Court decision, declaring that the Constitution of the United States does not permit a *State* to exclude slavery from its limits. And this may especially be expected if the doctrine of " care not whether slavery be voted down or voted up," shall gain upon the public mind sufficiently to give promise that such a decision can be maintained when made.

Such a decision is all that slavery now lacks of

being alike lawful in all the States. Welcome or unwelcome, such decision is probably coming, and will soon be upon us, unless the power of the present political dynasty, shall be met and overthrown. We shall lie down pleasantly dreaming that the people of Missouri are on the verge of making their State free, and we shall awake to the reality, instead, that the Supreme Court has made Illinois a slave State. To meet and overthrow that dynasty is the work before all those who would prevent that consummation. That is what we have to do. How can we best do it?

There are those who denounce us openly to their own friends, and yet whisper us softly that Senator Douglas is the aptest instrument there is with which to effect that object. They wish us to *infer* all, from the fact that he now has a little quarrel with the present head of the dynasty; and that he has regularly voted with us on a single point, upon which he and we have never differed. They remind us that he is a great man, and that the largest of us are very small ones. Let this be granted. "But a living dog is better than a dead lion." Judge Douglas, if not a dead lion, for this work, is at least a caged and toothless one. How can he

oppose the advances of slavery? He don't care
any thing about it. His avowed mission is im-
pressing the "public heart" to care nothing
about it. * * * Senator Douglas holds, we
know, that a man may rightfully be wiser to-day
than he was yesterday—that he may rightfully
change when he finds himself wrong. But can
we, for that reason, run ahead, and infer that he
will make any particular change, of which he
himself has given no intimation? Can we safely
base our action upon any such vague inference?
Now, as ever, I wish not to misrepresent Judge
Douglas' position, question his motives, or do
aught that can be personally offensive to him.
Whenever, if ever, he and we can come together on principle, so that our cause may have as-
sistance from his great ability, I hope to have in-
terposed no adventitious obstacle. But, clearly,
he is not now with us—he does not pretend to
be, he does not promise ever to be.

Our cause, then, must be entrusted to, and
conducted by its own undoubted friends—those
whose hands are free, whose hearts are in the
work—who *do care* for the result. Two years
ago the Republicans of the nation mustered over
thirteen hundred thousand strong. We did
this under the single impulse of resistance to a

common danger. With every external circum-
stance against us, of strange, discordant, and
even hostile elements, we gathered from the
four winds, and formed and fought the battle
through, under the constant hot fire of a disci-
plined, proud, and pampered enemy. Did we
brave all then, to falter now?—now, when that
same enemy is wavering, dissevered, and bel-
ligerent? The result is not doubtful. We shall
not fail—if we stand firm, we *shall not fail.*
Wise counsels may accelerate, or mistakes delay
it ; but, sooner or later, the victory is sure to
come.

STEPHEN ARNOLD DOUGLAS,

OF ILLINOIS.

(BORN 1813, DIED 1861.)

IN REPLY TO MR. LINCOLN ; FREEPORT, ILLS., AUGUST 27, 1858.

LADIES AND GENTLEMEN :

I am glad that at last I have brought Mr. Lincoln to the conclusion that he had better define his position on certain political questions to which I called his attention at Ottawa. * * * In a few moments I will proceed to review the answers which he has given to these interrogatories; but, in order to relieve his anxiety, I will first respond to those which he has presented to me. Mark you, he has not presented interrogatories which have ever received the sanction of the party with which I am acting, and hence he has no other foundation for them than his own curiosity.

First he desires to know, if the people of Kansas shall form a constitution by means entirely proper and unobjectionable, and ask admission as a State, before they have the requisite population for a member of Congress, whether I will vote for that admission. Well, now, I regret exceedingly that he did not answer that interrogatory himself before he put it to me, in order that we might understand, and not be left to infer, on which side he is. Mr. Trumbull, during the last session of Congress, voted from the beginning to the end against the admission of Oregon, although a free State, because she had not the requisite population for a member of Congress. Mr. Trumbull would not consent, under any circumstances, to let a State, free or slave, come into the Union until it had the requisite population. As Mr. Trumbull is in the field fighting for Mr. Lincoln, I would like to have Mr. Lincoln answer his own question and tell me whether he is fighting Trumbull on that issue or not. But I will answer his question. * * * Either Kansas must come in as a free State, with whatever population she may have, or the rule must be applied to all the other Territories alike. I therefore answer at once that, it having been decided that Kansas has people enough for a slave State, I hold that she has enough for a free State. I hope Mr. Lincoln is satisfied with my answer; and now I would like to get his answer to his own interrogatory—whether or not he will vote to admit Kansas before she has the requisite population. I want to know whether he will vote to admit Oregon before that Territory has the requisite population. Mr. Trumbull will not, and the same reason that commits Mr. Trumbull against the admission of Oregon commits him against Kansas, even if she should apply for admission as a free State. If there is any sincerity, any truth, in the argument of Mr. Trumbull in the Senate against the admission of Oregon, because she had not 93,420 people, although her population was larger than that of Kansas, he stands pledged against the admission of both Oregon and Kansas until they have 93,420 inhabitants. I would like Mr. Lincoln to answer this question. I would like him to take his own medicine. If he differs with Mr. Trumbull, let him answer his argument against the admission of Oregon, instead of poking questions at me.

The next question propounded to me by Mr. Lincoln is, Can the people of the Territory in any lawful way, against the wishes of any citizen of the United States, exclude slavery from their limits prior to the formation of a State Constitution? I answer emphatically, as Mr. Lincoln has heard me answer a hundred times from every stump in Illinois, that in my opinion the people of a Territory *can*, by lawful means, exclude slavery from their limits prior to the formation of a State Constitution. Mr. Lincoln knew that I had answered that question over and over again. He heard me argue the Nebraska bill on that principle all over the State in 1854, in 1855, and in 1856; and he has no excuse for pretending to be in doubt as to my position on that question. It matters not what way the Supreme Court may hereafter decide as to the abstract question whether slavery may or may not go into a Territory under the Constitution; the people have the lawful means to introduce it or exclude it as they please, for the reason that slavery cannot exist a day or an hour anywhere unless it is supported by local police regulations. Those police regulations can only be established by the local Legislature; and, if the people are opposed to slavery, they will elect representatives to that body who will by unfriendly legislation effectually prevent the introduction of it into their midst. If, on the contrary, they are for it, their legislation will

favor its extension.   Hence, no matter what the
decision of the Supreme Court may be on that
abstract question, still the right of the people
to make a slave Territory or a free Territory is
perfect and complete under the Nebraska bill.
I hope Mr. Lincoln deems my answer satisfac-
tory on that point.

In this connection, I will notice the charge
which he has introduced in relation to Mr.
Chase's amendment.   I thought that I had chased
that amendment out of Mr. Lincoln's brain at
Ottawa; but it seems that it still haunts his im-
agination, and that he is not yet satisfied.   I had
supposed that he would be ashamed to press
that question further.   He is a lawyer, and has
been a member of Congress, and has occu-
pied his time and amused you by telling you
about parliamentary proceedings.   He ought to
have known better than to try to palm off his
miserable impositions upon this intelligent
audience.   The Nebraska bill provided that the
legislative power and authority of the said Territory should extend to all rightful subjects of
legislation, consistent with the organic act and
the Constitution of the United States.   It
did not make any exception as to slavery,
but gave all the power that it was possible

for Congress to give, without violating the
Constitution, to the Territorial Legislature, with
no exception or limitation on the subject of
slavery at all.   The language of that bill, which
I have quoted, gave the full power and the fuller
authority over the subject of slavery, affirma-
tively and negatively, to introduce it or exclude
it, so far as the Constitution of the United States
would permit.   What more could Mr. Chase
give by his amendment?   Nothing!   He offered
his amendment for the identical purpose for
which Mr. Lincoln is using it, to enable dema-
gogues in the country to try and deceive the people.   His amendment was to this effect.   It
provided that the Legislature should have power
to exclude slavery ; and General Cass suggested:
" Why not give the power to introduce as well as
to exclude?"   The answer was—they have the
power already in the bill to do both.   Chase
was afraid his amendment would be adopted if
he put the alternative proposition, and so made
it fair both ways, and would not yield.   He offered it for the purpose of having it rejected.
He offered it, as he has himself avowed over
and over again, simply to make capital out of
it for the stump.   He expected that it would
be capital for small politicians in the coun-

try, and that they would make an effort to
deceive the people with it ; and he was not mistaken, for Lincoln is carrying out the plan
admirably.   *   *   *

The third question which Mr. Lincoln presented is—If the Supreme Court of the United
States shall decide that a State of this Union
cannot exclude slavery from its own limits, will
I submit to it ?   I am amazed that Mr. Lincoln
should ask such a question.   Mr. Lincoln's object is to cast an imputation upon the Supreme
Court.   He knows that there never was but one
man in America, claiming any degree of intelligence or decency, who ever for a moment pretended such a thing.   It is true that the Wash-
ington *Union,* in an article published on the 17th
of last December, did put forth that doctrine,
and I denounced the article on the floor of the
Senate.   *   *   *   Lincoln's friends, Trumbull,
and Seward, and Hale, and Wilson, and the
whole Black Republican side of the Senate were
silent.   They left it to me to denounce it.   And
what was the reply made to me on that occasion ?
Mr. Toombs, of Georgia, got up and undertook
to lecture me on the ground that I ought not to
have deemed the article worthy of notice, and
ought not to have replied to it ; that there was

not one man, woman, or child south of the Potomac, in any slave State, who did not repudiate any such pretension.   Mr. Lincoln knows that reply was made on the spot, and yet now he asks this question!   He might as well ask me—Suppose Mr. Lincoln should steal a horse, would I sanction it ; and it would be as genteel in me to ask him, in the event he stole a horse, what ought to be done with him.   He casts an imputation upon the Supreme Court of the United States, by supposing that they would violate the Constitution of the United States. I tell him that such a thing is not possible.   It would be an act of moral treason that no man on the bench could ever descend to.   Mr. Lincoln himself would never, in his partisan feelings, so far forget what was right as to be guilty of such an act.

The fourth question of Mr. Lincoln is—Are you in favor of acquiring additional territory in disregard as to how such acquisition may affect the Union on the slavery question ?   This question is very ingeniously and cunningly put. The Black Republican crowd lays it down expressly that under no circumstances shall we acquire any more territory unless slavery is first prohibited in the country.   I ask Mr. Lincoln

whether he is in favor of that proposition? Are
you opposed to the acquisition of any more
territory, under any circumstances, unless
slavery is prohibited in it? That he does not
like to answer. When I ask him whether he
stands up to that article in the platform of his
party, he turns, Yankee fashion, and, without
answering it, asks me whether I am in favor of
acquiring territory without regard to how it
may affect the Union on the slavery question.
I answer that, whenever it becomes necessary,
in our growth and progress, to acquire more
territory, I *am* in favor of it without reference
to the question of slavery, and when we have
acquired it, I will leave the people free to do as
they please, either to make it slave or free
territory, as they prefer. It is idle to tell me or
you that we have territory enough. * * *
With our natural increase, growing with a
rapidity unknown in any other part of the globe,
with the tide of emigration that is fleeing from
despotism in the old world to seek refuge in our
own, there is a constant torrent pouring into
this country that requires more land, more territory upon which to settle; and just as fast as
our interest and our destiny require additional
territory in the North, in the South, or in the

islands of the ocean, I am for it, and, when we acquire it, will leave the people, according to the Nebraska bill, free to do as they please on the subject of slavery and every other question.

I trust now that Mr. Lincoln will deem himself answered on his four points. He racked his brain so much in devising these four questions that he exhausted himself, and had not strength enough to invent the others. As soon as he is able to hold a council with his advisers, Lovejoy, Farnsworth, and Fred Douglas, he will frame and propound others ("Good," "good!"). You Black Republicans who say "good," I have no doubt, think that they are all good men. I have reason to recollect that some people in this country think that Fred Douglas is a very good man. The last time I came here to make a speech, while talking from a stand to you, people of Freeport, as I am doing to-day, I saw a carriage, and a magnificent one it was, drive up and take a position on the outside of the crowd; a beautiful young lady was sitting on the box seat, whilst Fred Douglas and her mother reclined inside, and the owner of the carriage acted as driver. I saw this in your own town. ("What of it?") All I have to say of it is this, that if you Black Republicans think that the negro ought to be on a social equality with your wives and daughters, and ride in a carriage with your wife, whilst you drive the team, you have a perfect right to do so. I am told that one of Fred Douglas' kinsmen, another rich black negro, is now travelling in this part of the State making speeches for his friend Lincoln as the champion of black men. ("What have you to say against it?") All I have to say on that subject is, that those of you who believe that the negro is your equal, and ought to be on an equality with you socially, politically, and legally, have a right to entertain those opinions, and of course will vote for Mr. Lincoln.

JOHN CALEB BRECKENRIDGE.

OF KENTUCKY.

(BORN 1821, DIED 1875.)

———

ON THE DRED SCOTT DECISION, BEFORE THE KENTUCKY LEGISLATURE, DECEMBER, 1859.

THE election took place on Monday. The day before I received a letter signed by a number of gentlemen in the Legislature asking my opinion in reference to the Dred Scott decision, in reference to Territorial sovereignty and the power of Congress to protect the property of citizens within the Territories. I received that letter with profound respect, and only regret that it did not come to my hands in time, that I might answer it before the election. * * *

Gentlemen, I bow to the decision of the Supreme Court of the United States upon every question within its proper jurisdiction, whether it corresponds with my private opinion or not; only, I bow a trifle lower when it happens to do so, as the decision in this Dred Scott case does.

I approve it in all its parts as a sound exposi-
tion of the law and constitutional rights of the
States, and citizens that inhabit them.

* * * I was in the Congress of the United
States when that Missouri line was repealed. I
never would have voted for any bill organizing
the Territory of Kansas as long as that odious
stigma upon our institutions remained upon the
statute book. I voted cheerfully for its repeal,
and in doing that I cast no reflection upon the
wise patriots who acquiesced in it at the time it
was established. It was repealed, and we
passed the act known as the Kansas-Nebraska
bill. The Abolition, or *quasi* Abolition, party
of the United States were constantly contend-
ing that it was the right of Congress to prohibit
slavery in the common Territories of the Union.
The Democratic party, aided by most of the
gentlemen from the South, took the opposite
view of the case. Our object was, if possible,
to withdraw that question from the halls of
Congress, and place it where it could no longer
risk the public welfare and the public interest. * * * There was a point upon which
we could not agree. A considerable portion of
the Northern Democracy held that slavery was
in derogation of common right, and could only

Legislatures, authorities created by Congress, had not the power to exclude or confiscate slave property, I confess that I had not anticipated that the doctrine of " unfriendly legislation " would be set up.   Hence I need not say to you that I do not believe in the doctrine of unfriendly legislation; that I do not believe in the authority of the Territorial Legislatures to do by indirection what they cannot do directly. I repose upon the decision of the Supreme Court of the United States, as to the point that neither Congress nor the Territorial Legislature has the right to obstruct or confiscate the property of any citizen, slaves included, pending the Territorial condition.   I do not see any escape from that decision, if you admit that the question was a judicial one; if you admit the decision of the Supreme Court; and if you stand by the decision of the highest court of the country.   The Supreme Court seems to have recognized it as the duty—*as the duty*—of the courts of this Union in their proper sphere to execute this constitutional right, thus adjudicated by the Supreme Court, in the following language :   *   *   *   " The judicial department is also bound *   *   *   to maintain in the Territory *   *   * the political rights and rights of property of individual citizens as secured by the Constitution." So that, in regard to slave property, as in regard to any other property recognized and guarded by the Constitution, it is the duty, according to the Supreme Court, of all the courts of the country to protect and guard it by their decisions, whenever the question is brought before them. To which I will only add this—that the judicial decisions in our favor must be maintained—these judicial decisions in our favor must be sustained.

WM. H. SEWARD,

OF NEW YORK.

(BORN 1801, DIED 1872.)

ON THE IRREPRESSIBLE CONFLICT; ROCHESTER, OCTOBER 25, 1858.

THE unmistakable outbreaks of zeal which occur all around me, show that you are earnest men—and such a man am I. Let us therefore, at least for a time, pass all secondary and collateral questions, whether of a personal or of a general nature, and consider the main subject of the present canvass. The Democratic party, or, to speak more accurately, the party which wears that attractive name—is in possession of the Federal Government. The Republicans propose to dislodge that party, and dismiss it from its high trust.

The main subject, then, is, whether the Democratic party deserves to retain the confidence of the American people. In attempting to prove it unworthy, I think that I am not actu-

ated by prejudices against that party, or by pre-
possessions in favor of its adversary; for I have
learned, by some experience, that virtue and
patriotism, vice and selfishness, are found in all
parties, and that they differ less in their motives
than in the policies they pursue.

Our country is a theatre, which exhibits, in
full operation, two radically different political
systems; the one resting on the basis of servile
or slave labor, the other on voluntary labor
of freemen. The laborers who are enslaved
are all negroes, or persons more or less purely
of African derivation. But this is only accidental. The principle of the system is, that labor in every society, by whomsoever performed,
is necessarily unintellectual, grovelling and base;
and that the laborer, equally for his own good
and for the welfare of the State, ought to be
enslaved. The white laboring man, whether
native or foreigner, is not enslaved, only because
he cannot, as yet, be reduced to bondage.

You need not be told now that the slave system is the older of the two, and that once it was
universal. The emancipation of our own ances-
tors, Caucasians and Europeans as they were,
hardly dates beyond a period of five hundred
years. The great melioration of human society

which modern times exhibit, is mainly due to the incomplete substitution of the system of voluntary labor for the one of servile labor, which has already taken place. This African slave system is one which, in its origin and in its growth, has been altogether foreign from the habits of the races which colonized these States, and established cizilization here. It was introduced on this continent as an engine of conquest, and for the establishment of monarchical power, by the Portuguese and the Spaniards, and was rapidly extended by them all over South America, Central America, Louisiana, and Mexico. Its legitimate fruits are seen in the poverty, imbecility, and anarchy which now pervade all Portuguese and Spanish America. The free-labor system is of German extraction, and it was established in our country by emigrants from Sweden, Holland, Germany, Great Britain and Ireland. We justly ascribe to its influences the strength, wealth, greatness, intelligence, and freedom, which the whole American people now enjoy. One of the chief elements of the value of human life is freedom in the pursuit of happiness. The slave system is not only intolerable, unjust, and inhuman, toward the laborer, whom, only because he is a laborer, it loads down with chains and converts into merchandise, but is scarcely less severe upon the freeman, to whom, only because he is a laborer from necessity, it denies facilities for employment, and whom it expels from the community because it cannot enslave and convert into merchandise also. It is necessarily improvident and ruinous, because, as a general truth, communities prosper and flourish, or droop and decline, in just the degree that they practise or neglect to practise the primary duties of justice and humanity. The free-labor system conforms to the divine law of equality, which is written in the hearts and consciences of man, and therefore is always and everywhere beneficent.

The slave system is one of constant danger, distrust, suspicion, and watchfulness. It debases those whose toil alone can produce wealth and resources for defence, to the lowest degree of which human nature is capable, to guard against mutiny and insurrection, and thus wastes energies which otherwise might be employed in national development and aggrandizement.

The free-labor system educates all alike, and by opening all the fields of industrial employment and all the departments of authority, to the

unchecked and equal rivalry of all classes of men,
at once secures. universal contentment, and
brings into the highest possible activity all the
physical, moral, and social energies of the whole
state. In states where the slave system prevails, the masters, directly or indirectly, secure
all political power, and constitute a ruling
aristocracy. In states where the free-labor system prevails, universal suffrage necessarily ob-
tains, and the state inevitably becomes, sooner
or later, a republic or democracy.

Russia yet maintains slavery, and is a despotism. Most of the other European states
have abolished slavery, and adopted the system of free labor. It was the antagonistic
political tendencies of the two systems which
the first Napoleon was contemplating when he
predicted that Europe would ultimately be
either all Cossack or all republican. Never did
human sagacity utter a more pregnant truth.
The two systems are at once perceived to be
incongruous. But they are more than incongruous—they are incompatible. They never
have permanently existed together in one
country, and they never can. It would be
easy to demonstrate this impossibility, from the
irreconcilable contrast between their great

principles and characteristics. But the experience of mankind has conclusively established
it. Slavery, as I have already intimated, existed
in every state in Europe. Free labor has sup-
planted it everywhere except in Russia and
Turkey. State necessities developed in modern
times are now obliging even those two nations
to encourage and employ free labor; and
already, despotic as they are, we find them en-
gaged in abolishing slavery. In the United
States, slavery came into collision with free
labor at the close of the last century, and fell
before it in New England, New York, New
Jersey, and Pennsylvania, but triumphed over it
effectually, and excluded it for a period yet un-
determined, from Virginia, the Carolinas, and
Georgia. Indeed, so incompatible are the two
systems, that every new State which is organized
within our ever-extending domain makes its
first political act a choice of the one and the ex-
clusion of the other, even at the cost of civil
war, if necessary. The slave States, without
law, at the last national election, successfully
forbade, within their own limits, even the cast-
ing of votes for a candidate for President of the
United States supposed to be favorable to the
establishment of the free-labor system in new
States.

Hitherto, the two systems have existed in different States, but side by side within the American Union. This has happened because the Union is a confederation of States. But in another aspect the United States constitute only one nation. Increase of population, which is filling the States out to their very borders, together with a new and extended net-work of railroads and other avenues, and an internal commerce which daily becomes more intimate, is rapidly bringing the States into a higher and more perfect social unity or consolidation. Thus, these antagonistic systems are continually coming into closer contact, and collision results.

Shall I tell you what this collision means? They who think that it is accidental, unnecessary, the work of interested or fanatical agitators, and therefore ephemeral, mistake the case altogether. It is an irrepressible conflict between opposing and enduring forces, and it means that the United States must and will, sooner or later, become either entirely a slave-holding nation, or entirely a free-labor nation. Either the cotton- and rice-fields of South Carolina and the sugar plantations of Louisiana will ultimately be tilled by free-labor, and Charleston and New Orleans become marts of legitimate merchandise alone, or else the rye-fields and wheat-fields of Massachusetts and New York must again be surrendered by their farmers to slave culture and to the production of slaves, and Boston and New York become once more markets for trade in the bodies and souls of men. It is the failure to apprehend this great truth that induces so many unsuccessful attempts at final compromises between the slave and free States, and it is the existence of this great fact that renders all such pretended compromises, when made, vain and ephemeral. Startling as this saying may appear to you, fellow-citizens, it is by no means an original or even a modern one. Our forefathers knew it to be true, and unanimously acted upon it when they framed the Constitution of the United States. They regarded the existence of the servile system in so many of the States with sorrow and shame, which they openly confessed, and they looked upon the collision between them, which was then just revealing itself, and which we are now accustomed to deplore, with favor and hope. They knew that one or the other system must exclusively prevail.

Unlike too many of those who in modern

time invoke their authority, they had a choice between the two. They preferred the system of free labor, and they determined to organize the government, and so direct its activity, that that system should surely and certainly prevail. For this purpose, and no other, they based the whole structure of the government broadly on the principle that all men are created equal, and therefore free—little dreaming that, within the short period of one hundred years, their descendants would bear to be told by any orator, however popular, that the utterance of that principle was merely a rhetorical rhapsody; or by any judge, however venerated, that it was attended by mental reservation, which rendered it hypocritical and false. By the ordinance of 1787, they dedicated all of the national domain not yet polluted by slavery to free labor immediately, thenceforth and forever; while by the new Constitution and laws they invited foreign free labor from all lands under the sun, and interdicted the importation of African slave labor, at all times, in all places, and under all circumstances whatsoever. It is true that they necessarily and wisely modified this policy of freedom by leaving it to the several States, affected as they were by different circumstances, to abolish slavery in their own way and at their own pleasure, instead of confiding that duty to Congress; and that they secured to the slave States, while yet retaining the system of slavery, a three-fifths representation of slaves in the Federal Government, until they should find themselves able to relinquish it with safety. But the very nature of these modifications fortifies my position, that the fathers knew that the two systems could not endure within the Union, and expected within a short period slavery would disappear forever. Moreover, in order that these modifications might not altogether defeat their grand design of a republic maintaining universal equality, they provided that two thirds of the States might amend the Constitution.

It remains to say on this point only one word, to guard against misapprehension. If these States are to again become universally slaveholding, I do not pretend to say with what violations of the Constitution that end shall be accomplished. On the other hand, while I do confidently believe and hope that my country will yet become a land of universal freedom, I do not expect that it will be made so otherwise than through the action of the several States

coöperating with the Federal Government, and
all acting in strict conformity with their respective constitutions.

The strife and contentions concerning slavery,
which gently-disposed persons so habitually
deprecate, are nothing more that the ripening
of the conflict which the fathers themselves not
only thus regarded with favor, but which they
may be said to have instituted.

* * * I know—few, I think, know better
than I—the resources and energies of the Democratic party, which is identical with the slave
power. I do ample justice to its traditional
popularity. I know further—few, I think, know
better than I—the difficulties and disadvan-
tages of organizing a new political force, like
the Republican party, and the obstacles it must
encounter in laboring without prestige and
without patronage. But, understanding all
this, I know that the Democratic party must go
down, and that the Republican party must rise
into its place. The Democratic party derived
its strength, originally, from its adoption of the
principles of equal and exact justice to all men.
So long as it practised this principle faithfully,
it was invulnerable. It became vulnerable when
it renounced the principle, and since that time

it has maintained itself, not by virtue of its own strength, or even of its traditional merits, but because there as yet had appeared in the political field no other party that had the conscience and the courage to take up, and avow, and practise the life-inspiring principle which the Democratic party had surrendered. At last, the Republican party has appeared. It avows, now, as the Republican party of 1800 did, in one word, its faith and its works, " Equal and exact justice to all men." Even when it first entered the field, only half organized, it struck a blow which only just failed to secure complete and triumphant victory. In this, its second campaign, it has already won advantages which render that triumph now both easy and certain.

The secret of its assured success lies in that very characteristic which, in the mouth of scoffers, constitutes its great and lasting imbecility and reproach. It lies in the fact that it is a party of one idea; but that is a noble one—an idea that fills and expands all generous souls; the idea of equality—the equality of all men before human tribunals and human laws, as they all are equal before the Divine tribunal and Divine laws.

I know, and you know, that a revolution has begun. I know, and all the world knows, that revolutions never go backward. Twenty Senators and a hundred Representatives proclaim boldly in Congress to-day sentiments and opinions and principles of freedom which hardly so many men, even in this free State, dared to utter in their own homes twenty years ago. While the Government of the United States, under the conduct of the Democratic party, has been all that time surrendering one plain and castle after another to slavery, the people of the United States have been no less steadily and perseveringly gathering together the forces with which to recover back again all the fields and all the castles which have been lost, and to confound and overthrow, by one decisive blow, the betrayers of the Constitution and freedom forever.

VI.

SECESSION.

VI.

SECESSION.

FROM the beginning of our history it has been a mooted question whether we are to consider the United States as a political state or as a congeries of political states, as a *Bundesstaat* or as a *Staatenbund.* The essence of the controversy seems to be contained in the very title of the republic, one school laying stress on the word United, as the other does on the word States. The phases of the controversy have been beyond calculation, and one of its consequences has been a civil war of tremendous energy and cost in blood and treasure.

Looking at the facts alone of our history, one would be most apt to conclude that the United States had been a political state from the beginning, its form being entirely revolutionary until the final ratification of the Articles of Confederation in 1781, then under the very loose and inefficient government of the Articles until 1789, and thereafter under the very efficient national government of the Constitution; that, in the final transformation of 1787-9, there were features which were also decidedly revolutionary; but that there was no time when any of the colonies had the prospect or the power of establishing a separate national existence of its own. The facts are not consistent with the theory that the States ever were independent political states, in any scientific sense.

It cannot be said, however, that the actors in the history always had a clear perception of the facts as they took place. In the teeth of the facts, our early history presents a great variety of assertions of State independence by leading men, State Legislatures, or State constitutions, which still form the basis of the argument for State sovereignty. The State constitutions declared the State to be sovereign and independent, even though the framers knew that the existence of the State depended on the issue of the national struggle against the mother . country. The treaty of 1783 with Great Britain recognized the States separately and by name as "free, sovereign, and independent," even while it established national boundaries outside of the States, covering a vast western territory in which no State would have ventured to forfeit its interest by setting up a claim to practical freedom, sovereignty, or independence. All our early history is full of such contradictions between fact and theory. They are largely obscured by the undiscriminating use of the word "people." As used now, it usually means the national people; but many apparently national phrases as to the "sovereignty of the people," as they were used in 1787–9, would seem far less national if the phraseology could show the feeling of those who then used them that the "people" referred to was the people of the State. In that case the number of the contradictions would be indefinitely increased; and the phraseology of the Constitu-

tion's preamble, " We, the people of the United
. States," would not be offered as a consciously
nationalizing phrase of its framers. It is hardly
to be doubted, from the current debates, that
the conventions of Massachusetts, New Hamp-
shire, Rhode Island, New York, Virginia, North
Carolina, and South Carolina, seven of the thirteen States, imagined and assumed that each
ratified the Constitution in 1788–90 by authority of the State's people alone, by the
State's sovereign will; while the facts show
that in each of these conventions a clear majority was coerced into ratification by a strong
minority in its own State, backed by the unani-
mous ratifications of the other States. If ratification or rejection had really been open to
voluntary choice, to sovereign will, the Constitution would never have had a moment's
chance of life; so far from being ratified by
nine States as a condition precedent to going
into effect, it would have been summarily rejected by a majority of the States. In the language of John Adams, the Constitution was

" extorted from the grinding necessities of a reluctant people." The theory of State sovereignty was successfully contradicted by national necessities.

The change from the Articles of Confederation to the Constitution, though it could not help antagonizing State sovereignty, was carefully managed so as to do so as little as possible. As soon as the plans by which the Federal party, under Hamilton's leadership, proposed to develop the national features of the Constitution became evident, the latent State feeling took fire. Its first symptom was the adoption of the name Republican by the new opposition party which took form in 1792–3 under Jefferson's leadership. Up to this time the States had been the only means through which Americans had known any thing of republican government; they had had no share in the government of the mother country in colonial times, and no efficient national government to take part in under the Articles of Confederation. The claim of an exclusive title to the name of

Republican does not seem to have been fundamentally an implication of monarchical tendencies against the Federalists so much as an implication that they were hostile to the States, the familiar exponents of republican government. When the Federalist majority in Congress forced through, in the war excitement against France in 1798, the Alien and Sedition laws, which practically empowered the President to suppress all party criticism of and opposition to the dominant party, the Legislatures of Kentucky and Virginia, in 1798–9, passed series of resolutions, prepared by Jefferson and Madison respectively, which for the first time asserted in plain terms the sovereignty of the States. The two sets of resolutions agreed in the assertion that the Constitution was a " compact," and that the States were the " parties " which had formed it. In these two propositions lies the gist of State sovereignty, of which all its remotest consequences are only natural developments. If it were true that the States, of their sovereign will, had formed such a compact; if it were not true that the adoption of the Constitution was a mere alteration of the form of a political state already in existence; it would follow, as the Kentucky resolutions asserted, that each State had the exclusive right to decide for itself when the compact had been broken, and the mode and measure of redress. It followed, also, that, if the existence and force of the Constitution in a State were due solely to the sovereign will of the State, the sovereign will of the State was competent, on occasion, to oust the Constitution from the jurisdiction covered by the State. In brief, the Union was wholly voluntary in its formation and in its continuance; and each State reserved the unquestionable right to secede, to abandon the Union, and assume an independent existence whenever due reason, in the exclusive judgment of the State, should arise. These latter consequences, not stated in the Kentucky resolutions, and apparently not contemplated by the Virginia resolutions, were put into complete form by Professor Tucker, of

the University of Virginia, in 1803, in the notes
to his edition of " Blackstone's Commentaries."
Thereafter its statements of American constitutional law controlled the political training of
the South.

Madison held a modification of the State
sovereignty theory, which has counted among its
adherents the mass of the ability and influence
of American authorities on constitutional law.
Holding that the Constitution was a compact,
and that the States were the parties to it, he
held that one of the conditions of the compact
was the abandonment of State sovereignty;
that the States were sovereign until 1787-8, but
thereafter only members of a political state,
the United States. This seems to have been
the ground taken by Webster, in his debates
with Hayne and Calhoun. It was supported
by the instances in which the appearance of a
sovereignty in each State was yielded in the
fourteen years before 1787 ; but, unfortunately
for the theory, Calhoun was able to produce instances exactly parallel after 1787. If the fact

that each State predicated its own sovereignty as an essential part of the steps preliminary to the convention of 1787 be a sound argument for State sovereignty before 1787, the fact that each State predicated its sovereignty as an essential part of the ratification of the Constitution must be taken as an equally sound argument for State sovereignty under the Constitution; and it seems difficult, on the Madison theory, to resist Calhoun's triumphant conclusion that, if the States went into the convention as sovereign States, they came out of it as sovereign States, with, of course, the right of secession. Calhoun himself had a sincere desire to avoid the exercise of the right of secession, and it was as a substitute for it that he evolved his doctrine of nullification, which has been placed in the first volume. When it failed in 1833, the exercise of the right of secession was the only remaining remedy for an asserted breach of State sovereignty.

The events which led up to the success of the Republican party in electing Mr. Lincoln to the

Presidency in 1860 are so intimately connected
with the antislavery struggle that they have
been placed in the preceding volume. They
culminated in the first organized attempt to
put the right of secession to a practical test.
The election of Lincoln, the success of a "sec-
tional party," and the evasion of the fugitive-
slave law through the passage of "personal-lib-
erty laws" by many of the Northern States,
are the leading reasons assigned by South Carolina for her secession in 1860. These were in-
telligible reasons, and were the ones most com-
monly used to influence the popular vote. But
all the evidence goes to show that the leaders
of secession were not so weak in judgment as
to run the hazards of war by reason of "inju-
ries" so minute as these. Their apprehensions
were far broader, if less calculated to influence
a popular vote. In 1789 the proportions of
population and wealth in the two sections were
very nearly equal. The slave system of labor
had hung as a clog upon the progress of the
South, preventing the natural development of

manufactures and commerce, and shutting out immigration. As the numerical disproportion between the two sections increased, Southern leaders ceased to attempt to control the House of Representatives, contenting themselves with balancing new Northern with new Southern States, so as to keep an equal vote in the Senate. Since 1845 this resource had failed. Five free States, Iowa, Wisconsin, California, Minnesota, and Oregon, had been admitted, with no new slave States; Kansas was calling almost imperatively for admission; and there was no hope of another slave State in future. When the election of 1860 demonstrated that the progress of the antislavery struggle had united all the free States, it was evident that it was but a question of time when the Republican party would control both branches of Congress and the Presidency, and have the power to make laws according to its own interpretation of the constitutional powers of the Federal Government.

The peril to slavery was not only the probable prohibition of the inter-State slave-trade, though this itself would have been an event which negro slavery in the South could hardly have long survived. The more pressing danger lay in the results of such general Republican success on the Supreme Court. The decision of that Court in the Dred Scott case had fully sustained every point of the extreme Southern claims as to the status of slavery in the Territories; it had held that slaves were property in the view of the Constitution; that Congress was bound to protect slave-holders in this property right in the Territories, and, still more, bound not to prohibit slavery or allow a Territorial Legislature to prohibit slavery in the Territories, and that the Missouri compromise of 1820 was unconstitutional and void. The Southern Democrats entered the election of 1860 with this distinct decision of the highest judicial body of the country to back them. The Republican party had refused to admit that the decision of the Dred Scott case was law or binding. Given a Republican majority in both Houses and a Republican President, there was nothing to hinder the passage of a law increasing the number of Supreme Court justices to any desired extent, and the new appointments would certainly be of such a nature as to make the reversal of the Dred Scott decision an easy matter. The election of 1860 had brought only a Republican President; the majority in both Houses was to be against him until 1863 at least. But the drift in the North and West was too plain to be mistaken, and it was felt that 1860-1 would be the last opportunity for the Gulf States to secede with dignity and with the prestige of the Supreme Court's support.

Finally, there seems to have been a strong feeling among the extreme secessionists, who loved the right of secession for its own sake, that the accelerating increase in the relative power of the North would soon make secession, on any grounds, impossible. Unless the right was to be forfeited by non-user, it must be established by practical exercise, and at once.

Until about 1825-9 Presidential electors were

www.ingramcontent.com/pod-product-compliance
Lightning Source LLC
Chambersburg PA
CBHW022152020726
47496CB00008B/2672